Duck Hunting on the Fox

Hunting & Decoy-Carving Traditions

Stephen M. Miller

photographs by Michael Brisson

PRAIRIE OAK PRESS

Black Earth, Wisconsin

Library of Congress Control Number: 2002105568
ISBN: 1-931599-13-0

Project Manager: Anne McKenna
Editor: Jerry Minnich
Book Design: John Huston
Cover Design: John Huston

All paintings by Milt Geyer. Reproduced with permission. All other art and photographs used
with permission; any unauthorized duplication is prohibited. For more information contact
the publisher.

Printing in China by Four Colour Imports

06 05 04 03 02   6 5 4 3 2 1

Prairie Oak Press, a division of Trails Media Group, Inc.
P.O. Box 317 • Black Earth, WI 53515
(800) 236-8088 • e-mail: books@wistrails.com
www.trailsbooks.com

Dedication

for my family,
for my hunting friends

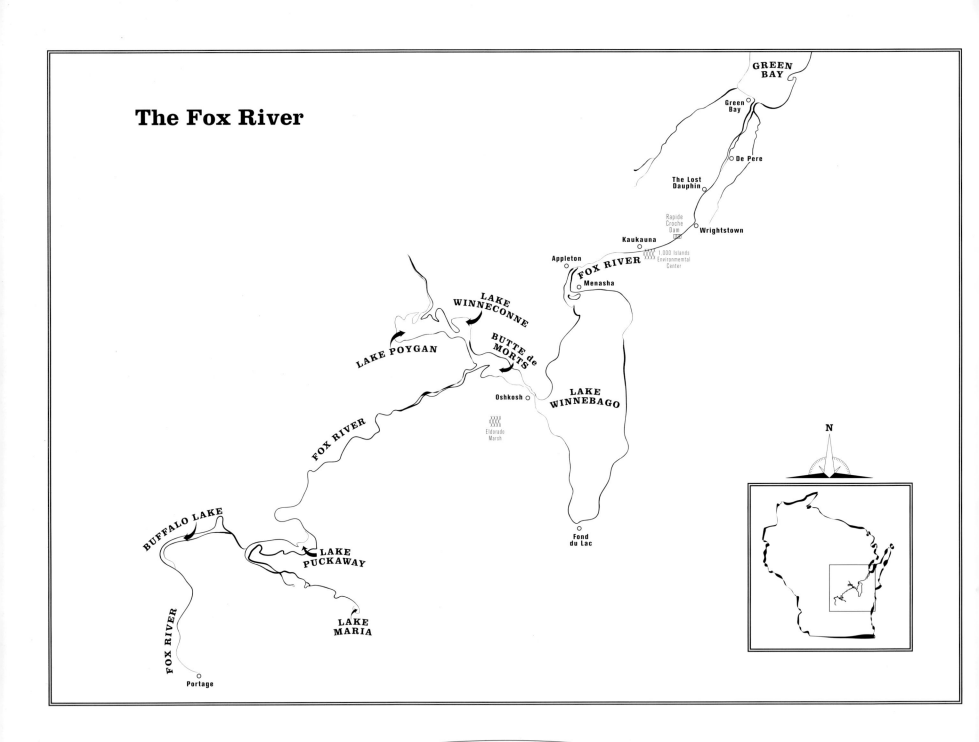

The Fox River

GREEN BAY

Green Bay

De Pere

The Lost Dauphin

Rapide Croche Dam

Wrightstown

Kaukauna

1,000 Islands Environmemtal Center

Appleton

FOX RIVER

Menasha

LAKE WINNECONNE

BUTTE de MORTS

LAKE POYGAN

LAKE WINNEBAGO

Oshkosh

FOX RIVER

Eldorado Marsh

Fond du Lac

BUFFALO LAKE

LAKE PUCKAWAY

FOX RIVER

LAKE MARIA

Portage

N

Contents

Acknowledgments

Thanks to Phil Martin, Jerry Minnich, and John Motoviloff for their help and encouragement. I thank the poetry editor of *Wisconsin Academy Review*, where many of the poems appeared in earlier versions. Also, I appreciate the assistance of Anita Lightfoot and Lee Strasheim. When interviewed, the hunters whose words appear here were in their seventies and eighties. Many have since passed away. They generously left their stories, inspiring future generations to leave warm beds before dawn to visit the magic of the duck marshes.

Duck skiff on Green Bay.

**Ted Thyrion and John Basteyns with their decoys
(fishing-net reel in background), Green Bay 1920s.**

Foreword

by Philip Martin

This book is about a place: the marshes of Green Bay and the reaches of the Fox River that empty into the bay. Hundreds of years ago, the Fox River was a favored route for early French explorers, who traveled in birchbark canoes from Mackinac Island on Lake Huron into Lake Michigan, following the south shore of the Upper Peninsula of Michigan into the shallow marshes of Green Bay. The French adventurers then paddled and poled their way up the Fox River to a point where, with a mercifully brief portage of canoes and heavy bundles of trade goods, they could refloat their fragile craft in the Wisconsin River. From there, a swift current sped them downriver to the heart of the interior: the watery highway of the mighty Mississippi.

Today, the Fox River is known far and wide for its paper mills. The river flows past industrial smokestacks of some of the nation's leading papermaking companies, from Green Bay to Kaukauna, Neenah, Menasha, and Appleton farther up the Fox.

The same river that once floated birchbark canoes and now irrigates the paper mills is also renowned to area hunters as a great spot for waterfowling. The geography of Green Bay acts as a great funnel, channeling vast flocks of migrating ducks and geese—winging down each autumn from the prairies of western Canada and the shores of Hudson Bay—into the narrowing bay and Fox River.

First, the birds stop to rest and feed on the end of Green Bay—a shallow spot whose great marshes, now diminished, once stretched endlessly along its shores. Then the migrating birds begin their journey up the Fox—a perilous flight, as the shores are lined in October and November with hunters.

Overhead fly the flocks of mallard, teal, bluebill, and canvasback. Underneath wait the hunters, reclining in floating skiffs on the marshes of the bay, sitting on seat cushions in river blinds, their decoys spread in careful patterns, duck calls ready, shotguns loaded, coffee thermoses close at hand.

Duck hunting is a practical pastime, a way to put food on the table. By and large, these marsh and river hunters were

working-class fellows: blue-collar employees of paper mills, shopkeepers, bricklayers, and auto mechanics. They were not the elite hunters of wealthy hunting clubs, who hired guides and rented rigs of fine decoys, who met afterward at the clubhouse to sip Scotch whiskey and send postcards home.

Instead, the Fox River hunters were guys who often carved their own decoys, built their own blinds, crafted their own skiffs. They shot birds and cleaned them to feed their families—especially through the lean years of the Depression. They didn't buy expensive decoys, or waste shotgun shells, because they couldn't afford to and didn't want to.

Yet duck hunting is also an artistic pursuit of sorts—although these hunters would never call themselves artists. They might tolerate another term: bearers of tradition. Clearly, duck hunting combines ritual and craft, from the carving of a wooden bird to the making of a skiff that rides the waves well, from the sharing of a good story to the richly detailed folk knowledge of weather, bird behavior, and customs of hunting in a particular marsh or river blind.

A few of the local hunters became specialists, like the legendary Frisque family of Green Bay who hunted only canvasback, nothing else. Most, however, were generalists; they shot anything edible. In season, they hunted deer, fished, trapped crabs, and hunted pheasant or grouse.

Is duck hunting a traditional art form or a practical pastime, everyday skill or ritual performance? Waterfowling has been compared by some outdoors writers to a special communion, a meeting with a celestial host to share some sacrifice of blood and flesh, an exchange marked by ritual and custom. The metaphor is rich and resonant with the ethnic-immigrant Catholic heritage of the Fox River Valley.

Duck Hunting on the Fox explores some of this through the simple magic of memories and small moments. Drawing on long lifetimes of hunting, elder hunters recall hunting the marshes of the bay and the twists and turns of the Fox. With color photography by Mike Brisson, an outdoors photographer with long experience in the region, the book also includes reminiscences by the author (an accomplished poet) of his own boyhood days as a young hunter growing up on the Fox.

An extra bonus is an appendix listing more than 30 historic decoy carvers of the region, with photographic examples of their work.

This book evokes the feeling of a hunt—the morning mist on the water, the whisper of wind through cattails, the waiting, the slowly rising sun, the calls of a descending flock—and the

Market hunters, Green Bay area, date unknown.

Redheads by Milt Geyer.

sharing of stories afterward with comrades of the hunt.

Sitting in a blind, or rocking gently in a skiff, is a timeless moment. It gives time to reflect on the amazing bounty of nature in her autumn glory, spread before the hunter's eyes. Less apparent, even (or especially) to those who do it, are the rich treasures of human culture, woven like a cattail screen into the ways of duck hunting.

Perhaps it would help to envision this heritage as a sort of "marshland of intangibles," where customs return each year to a favorite hunting spot like the ducks—where respect for tradition instructs a drawknife to make a decoy that floats well—where hunters behave in their blind as they were taught by older friends and neighbors, and tell good stories. Somehow these folkways help bring down the game as much as using the proper type of shotgun shell.

How can we understand that when folkways work, when traditions are "just right," everything fits together in a way that is more satisfying? It is not easy to see this actually happening. The diversity of a regional culture, like an impressionistic painting, shows little of its true meaning if the viewer is too close to the canvas. Only as you step slowly back does the picture come into focus.

Perhaps a better analogy, again, is a marsh—which you see only in small pieces but "know" in a greater whole, born of countless days spread over many seasons and years, with friends and alone, in wet weather and sunny, on days when nothing happens—and on the day that becomes a story to tell for half a century.

Like the wetlands so prized by duck hunters—staunch conservationists to the core—this rich heritage of regional lore also has great value. It is deeply rooted, precious, and not easily replaced. It is part of a web of life, connected to other patterns of nature and human behavior. And in some cases—like too many fine marshlands—our regional culture is endangered.

Who will maintain this lore after the old hunters pass on? Like all conservation efforts, the most effective start at the local level—when elders pause to instruct younger generations, when those who have the deep knowledge and wisdom, grown from long, slow times spent in one place, share their stories with those who are at least wise enough to listen.

Introduction

"We left this bay to enter a river emptying into it. It is very beautiful at its mouth, and flows gently; it is full of ... duck, teal, and other birds, attracted by the wild oats of which they are very fond."

—Father Claude Dablon writing of the voyages of Father James Marquette, 1679

Growing up near the waters of Green Bay and the Fox River generates many impressions. After awhile, one realizes it's the same thing said over and over—water is the center.

One of my earliest memories is being curled up on the rear window ledge of my parents' 1930s Chevrolet as we traveled the river road between Green Bay and Kaukauna, telephone lines dipping and flowing in twilight, Burma Shave signs, fields of brown grasses. The river always near.

When I was four or five years old and first saw it, the Green Bay Sanctuary was a wonder. Located minutes from downtown Green Bay, the sanctuary had a great horned owl behind chicken wire in a rough, wooden cage. And you could feed shelled corn to wild mallard, black ducks, and Canada geese.

Adventure on water is a common bond here. A postman I met was raised on the river. As a boy, he says, in spring he netted and speared suckers and carp, fish that his family would smoke. He walked the riverbanks from Kaukauna to Wrightstown, hunting squirrel, rabbit, puddle ducks. He remembers his grandmother telling one of the kids to go down to the river to catch four fish for the evening meal. The river had sheepshead, bullhead, yellow perch, northern pike, and walleye. In spring it flooded the field next to the local library: fish beside books.

It was not all a paradise. The mill emptied barrels with remnants of dye directly into the river; the water ran red. And in Wrightstown, raw sewage drifted by. Local ducks didn't taste as good as new birds coming down from Canada.

Thousand Islands, Kaukauna, on the Fox River, where several hundred hunters congregated on opening day of duck season in 1929.

My own recollections include spring nights on the river, building a bonfire on shore, and netting smelt in such number that they filled gunnysacks.

In summer, we'd go to the bay and rent wide, freshly painted wooden rowboats for a dollar a day at the Crows Nest Tavern. We'd row offshore, anchor, and fish for yellow perch. The hollow sound of bailing with a coffee can, the smell of hot sun on pine, the ragged touch of anchor rope. Some days my aunt, uncle, brother, and I would catch a hundred perch in an afternoon. Often perch bit best when a squall blew up from the north. We'd most always wait too long and then lift anchor (a metal can filled with concrete) as the oily, dark surface changed to whitecaps much too high for comfort. We'd row toward shore, certain that our chances of making land were worth a bent slug stuck in the coin slot of a Bay Beach Arcade amusement machine.

In autumn during the early 1950s, when I attended St. Francis Grade School in De Pere, boys talked about their fathers taking them on weekends to Green Bay's western shore, to the duck shacks. On some days fathers hunted the bay shore, leaving their sons to sit on the roofs of the shacks and shoot at teal and mallard that flew by. There were that many ducks.

Waterfowling was in the air, everywhere. Outdoors maga- zines carried pages of romantic, four-color art. On the newsstands were thick stacks of *Sports Afield Know Your Ducks and Geese*, with its evocative Angus Shortt paintings. An autumn issue of the then-new *Sports Illustrated* was heart- stopping with a photo essay showing decoys from the hand of carver Shang Wheeler and up-to-date reports about the duck migrations.

One could pick up the phone and hear recorded announce- ments from local sporting-goods stores about where the ducks were on the bay and the size of the flocks. Some congregations of bluebill, redhead, and canvasback were miles long.

A visit to any sporting-goods store brought you face-to-face with row upon row of decoys for sale: wooden canvasback by Wildfowler, papier-mâché bluebill by Carry-Lite, hollow plas- tic and foam mallard by any number of makers. There was the scent of tarred decoy cord. The dull sheen of lead keels and anchors for the decoys.

On September evenings, duck blinds burned on the river, where there was always competition for favorite points. Old-timers torched the blinds of newcomers who had overstepped and built too close on desirable locations already claimed by tradition.

At the east De Pere barbershop, conversation was about hunting below the Lost Dauphin's cabin on the river. Classmates who could borrow a car drove river roads in early morning, often coming to school with stories of bagging a helldiver (pied-billed grebe) or infrequently a mallard. Looking out of the window of my high school woodworking classroom, where I made profile black-duck decoys, I saw black-and-white bluebill ducks bobbing on the Fox River. On most any autumn weekend, great V-shaped spreads of wooden diving-duck decoys rode the river. It was like walking into a beautiful sporting print.

In 1953, when living on a farm, I reached up into the rafters of a chicken house and found an old 12-gauge single-shot shotgun. I went on my first hunts in Tomahawk, Wisconsin, and bagged grouse. The North Woods were exciting, but there was action closer to home, though it was difficult to reach without car, duck skiff, decoys, and hip boots. I saved my allowance and money from chores, bought three decoys, shotshells, and hip boots, and bicycled every chance I got to an old concrete blind at the edge of the east De Pere cemetery.

Today, the bay, the river, and its ducks and geese remain a constant against which to measure everything else. In any of the towns along the river or bay, ask a stranger, "Are geese coming through?" or "Do you know anyone who hunts ducks?" The reply is rich with helpful information.

I met Milt Geyer in the summer of 1982 at a decoy show sponsored by the Green Bay Duck Hunters Association. An elegant black-duck decoy was on one of the tables. I picked it up, turned it upside down, and read out loud the words carved on its flat bottom: "Milt Geyer, 1937." A voice said, "Yes?" I was holding a decoy carved 45 years earlier, my imagination locked into a time before I was born, but standing beside me was a youngish-acting man who had actually carved this bird.

That was the beginning of my friendship with one of the Midwest's finest decoy makers. Milt later introduced me to his "chum," Ted Thyrion. Ted is Milt's duck hunting companion, and also a decoy maker. A retired commercial fisherman, he and Milt team up each spring and summer to rescue abandoned broods of wild mallard in Green Bay.

Thirty miles south of Green Bay, as the canvasback flies, is the small town of Kaukauna with its Fox River marshes. Here, on a beautiful, green July morning in the 1970s, I met Jerome Kilgas, a retired paper mill worker. Jerome was making decoys in his garage, located a stone's throw from the home of Jacob

Miller. Jacob, my grandfather, was a saloon owner, a baseball and boxing expert, and a well-known duck hunter.

Jerome later introduced me to Bob Wurdinger, a retired river pilot, who took me to his blind on the river for two mornings of bluebill hunting in 1985, in the company of Bob's brother, Lowry, and Jerry Vils.

I saw Wally Mooney's decoys at the Kaukauna Environmental Center long before I met Wally. Like some of the other hunters whose stories appear here, Wally is a retired employee of the paper mills. Also, like many of the area's hunters, Wally is so involved with community projects that he's difficult to track down. At any given moment he might be inside a church setting up a public-address system, or carving a 16-foot totem pole for a Scout troop, or paddling across the river with his video camera to take pictures of nesting eagles, or creating a prairie at the Environmental Center. One day, while operating a cash register at the St. Vincent de Paul Secondhand Store, he told me about a hunt for goldeneye ducks when he tipped over his skiff when the temperature was four below zero.

The water is cleaner now in the river and bay than it was a few decades ago. Game fish are found in greater numbers.

There are nesting eagles. In winter, ice-fishing shanties are a common sight. In spring and summer, mallard hens with ducklings swim among water lilies. In October, there are rafts of feeding coot and bluebill. The diving ducks are fewer than they were 50 years ago, but in their place are great flocks of Canada geese.

I was in a parking lot at the Kimberly mall, recently, when the air filled with raucous honking. A few yards above, 11 geese broke through the fog. Two separated and went their own way, but the flock called louder until the pair flew back, and everything was again as orderly as nuns filing into church.

Is the lore of fishing, hunting, and decoy carving now only a memory? Fox River outdoorsman Bob Wurdinger answers the question as well as anyone when he tells about one flock of bluebill after another pouring into his decoys on a blustery November day. Forty to fifty ducks in a flock, says Bob. At one time there were two hundred bluebills swimming among his decoys. "When was that?" I asked, expecting the answer to be: "50 or 60 years ago." Bob said, "That shoot was six years ago."

Jack Schmitz on the bay near Suamico. Milt Geyer based his painting of a hunter on this photograph.

M

ary Ellen stands in green light, white canvas
crossing guard straps across her gray cotton jacket.
When I'm inside the blind, its leaning concrete walls
and the haze of autumn are the limits of the world.

This morning, Myrl and I hunt below the cabin of the lost
dauphin. Mallards stand on banks of mud. The mist holds
steady in drizzle as we steal through sopped cattails.
On the river, hundreds of them. Three others, wings
set like sickles, glide downward from the heavens.

The qua qua qua of a hen mallard echoes off maples.
A drake waddles down the flat into the bay, paddles off,
leaving a ripple like thread from a spool.

These shallows brim with wild celery, duckweed, snails,
unlike the sterile lakes up north where you wait
and see nothing. Gray-eyed Mary Ellen glows like the
painted robes of wooden statues from the fifteenth century,
like this river of purple, green, and shimmering birds.

Our shotguns fire but in this fog the ducks are more distant
than they appear. The greenhead mallard I shoot at steps down
from a snag. Myrl and I stand on the shore, exposed, shivering.

All morning we stalk and shoot at sitting gray ducks, teal,
swimming mudhens. We clip nary a feather. The fog vanishes
like an intake of breath. The red channel buoy is revealed,
then the tar road, a white baker truck. Morning removes
itself like paper slipped into a great, yellowing envelope.

—*Stephen Miller*

Capturing raindrops but no insects on an overcast October morning, a spider creates
his own hunt on the bank of the Fox River between Kaukauna and Wrightstown.

S1

SECTION ONE

THE BAY

Milt Geyer's Story

I was born on January 15, 1912, in Green Bay, and I began hunting when I was 16 years old. The first duck that I shot was a mallard, shot over decoys that I had made myself. Back then, the limit was 25 ducks, plus all the mudhen you wanted to shoot.

I lived on the east shore of Green Bay and hunted at Whitney Slough. We had a lot of canvasback around Green Bay at that time. On my best canvasback day, I shot three of them, but there were so many other ducks around that you didn't just pick canvasback. Oh, there used to be thousands of ducks around Green Bay when we had the marsh on the east and west shores.

There were many places to hunt back then. A lot of the marsh is washed out, now. Some of the hunting places were Little Tail Point, Long Tail Point, Baby Bass and Big Bass Channels, Peats Lake, Halfway Slough, Whitney Slough, and Deadhorse. Duck Creek was good, too.

When I was a youngster, I'd hunt every day when I was on vacation. Otherwise, I'd hunt only on weekends. On Fridays, I would go out on a date until midnight or one a.m., come home, change clothes, and then go out in the skiff. Then I would come home, eat supper, change clothes, go out on a date. Sunday morning, I'd be on the marsh, again.

I'd be pretty doggoned tired by the time Sunday night came along.

When I was a kid, I would pole my skiff out on the East River before dawn to Duck Creek. I'd use a push pole. I'd get to the creek just before dawn. Then, from the opposite direction would come a motor boat. All of the ducks would go up in waves.

I never hunted the Fox River. The fellows on the river did well on stormy days.

On the west bay shore, hunters would often stay put in their blinds until about nine o'clock. Then the ducks that they'd jumped out of the marsh would begin to come back. By this time, the hunters had come out of the marsh, too. So these were perfect times for me to jump in the skiff and go into the marsh, either jump shooting or with a few decoys.

My brother Ben and I would wait until eight o'clock to go into the marsh. Then we'd go out with a few decoys. The mallard would be returning. They'd fly in so high, turn, and then pitch into the potholes.

We hunt from skiffs. I bought one in Oconto Falls for 15 dollars. I bought another one for 50. The 50-dollar one weighs a hundred pounds. It's the skiff that I most generally hunt from.

There was one dangerous time. Once, on Grassy Island, I had a mile of water to cross. A northwest wind was at my back. Waves rolled over the back of the deck, along the combing, over the peak, and all that was sticking out of the water was the combing. She'd come up on a wave and go down. That's the only time I was scared.

We'd set out handmade, wooden-slat crab traps when we went hunting. If you didn't get ducks, you'd come back with crabs.

Ready for action on Green Bay's west shore, in the third week of October, when bluebill and mallard flights move down from Canada.

Milt Geyer heading out for a day in the marsh. No blind needed. Milt hunts from his skiff after backing it into cattails.

Surrounded by cattails, calling for greenhead, Milt Geyer sends out an invitation to high flyers trading above the bay's west shore.

A hand that shows wear from decades of carving decoys
and hunting in sleet and snow. Milt Geyer walks to a
secluded pothole in search of ingredients for mudhen stew.

There were three guys who owned a shack on the East River. Anytime they saw someone with a gun crossing the bridge, they'd ask for game. They'd eat groundhog, muskrat carcasses, shitepoke, all that stuff. Batching it, those three guys.

The marsh went about 20 years ago. It went because of pollution and because carp rooted it out. The marsh drifted out into the bay. It used to be the biggest hunting area north of Horicon Marsh National Wildlife Refuge. We had a lot of territory here. Now it's all gone. We still get ducks, don't get me wrong, but now they don't even come into the bay until the season is closed. The hunting seasons are short, now. You still see a lot of ducks here after the season closes.

You ask about rafts of ducks a mile or two in length during the 1950s. Oh, yah. In the morning, the boats would chase the ducks out of Duck Creek, and the sky would be just black with ducks. The ducks would get chased out of the bay. A lot of them would feed on Winnebago, Butte des Morts, and other lakes around here. There was a lot of feed around then.

Every evening the ducks would fly to Lake Winnebago, flock after flock after flock, for an hour and a half, over the Fox River on the way to Lake Winnebago. Then, in the morning, they'd fly back to Green Bay again.

I generally use 30 or 35 decoys when hunting with someone and a dozen or 15 when I'm hunting alone. I hunt with a Winchester Model 12. I have a 20-gauge Remington Model 870 and a double-barrel shotgun, too.

Jump shooting on the marsh is something that I mostly did when I was young. We had a cottage on the west shore of Green Bay. We'd sit on the boathouse with binoculars and watch the ducks come in, turn, and go back down into the marsh. Then we'd put on waders and go back into the marsh and jump the ducks up. That was great.

My best hunts? A couple times I limited out at 25 ducks. And mudhen, too. A good mudhen stew is really good if you know someone who knows how to cook it. Stew 'em with fresh vegetables, carrots, celery, onions, and so forth.

When I worked at the Bay West Paper Company, I'd always take my vacation at Thanksgiving, to hunt in areas that weren't iced in.

I'd hunt for mallards in the ice holes sometimes. Once, I set out three decoys and got into a flock of three mallard. I got the first two. The other turned around and flew back and I got that one, too.

Back then, a goose was something special to brag about. Now, of course, geese are common. Today, the geese you see are mostly Canadas. Occasionally a blue, snow, or cackler will be taken.

My favorite duck to hunt are mallard. They're good to eat and good to hunt. Teal and wood ducks are good tasting, as are canvasback. Bluebill (scaup) are not too bad, but I favor the other ducks.

Myron Frisque and his dad and Bill Merrick hunted together. They were great canvasback hunters. They hunted canvasback and never bothered with anything else, because canvasback were thick in those days. They'd go lay out in the reeds in the open water in the 1940s and 1950s.

There were a lot of black ducks in the 1940s. They're scarce now. A lot of them are in the Green Bay Sanctuary, but you never see young ones there. I don't know why that is.

There were more pintails back then, too. We used to have flocks of 25 to 30 come in.

Canvasbacks **by Milt Geyer.**

A rig of wooden bluebill on the bottom of Milt Geyer's duck skiff. The hook-ended stick in the background to the right helps to retrieve out-of-reach decoys.

Canada Geese by Milt Geyer.

Duck skiff by Dan Kidney Boat Works, made at De Pere on the Fox River. This is the Green Bay Model, designed for the open waters of the bay.

I've made 250 to 300 decoys, just counting the working decoys. Plus mantle decoys, loons, wood ducks, and teal. One woman bought a bufflehead for her husband as a wedding present. Most of the decoys that I make for hunting are mallard, bluebill, and canvasback.

I get a kick out of other hunters mistaking my decoys for wild ducks. Sometimes they sneak up and pepper my birds. I yell out, "Can't you tell ducks from decoys?" One guy shot a coot decoy that I'd set out, and it was swinging back and forth in the current of a creek. Boom! He didn't see me lying down in my boat in the reeds. The shot went over my head and hit the mudhen. "Can't you tell a mudhen decoy?" I said. He got so mad. He threw his hat into the bottom of his boat and paddled off.

I make my decoys with so many details because I like hunting over something that looks nice. I like seeing ducks come in, land, and tuck their heads under their wings and go to sleep. There have been times when I have paddled through my decoys and a live bird just stayed with the wooden ones.

Realistic birds bring the birds in close, which is what you need when you want ducks for the table.

I shot snipe only once. Fifteen lit on a sandbar. I got eight in one shot, but when I cooked them up, I found that I didn't like their taste.

The best days are gone. I try to do everything that I can to save what I can. Now, when ducks land in the decoys I often just watch them. Sometimes I'll shoot a drake. I let the females go.

The size of duck flocks today is mostly eight to ten in a flock. It's nicer to shoot at a flock this size than the bigger flocks. The biggest flock I ever had an opportunity at was when 50 bluebill landed. Twenty-five ducks were allowed, then, for a daily limit. I got four in one shot. I didn't shoot again.

Another time, nine bluewing teal came in. When they got above the decoys, I stood up. When they flared, I fired one shot, got five; fired twice more, and got one with each shot. Seven out of nine. That's the most I ever got out of one bunch. When you get teal and put dressing in them and roast them, boy, are they delicious!

At one place on the east shore of the bay, ruddy ducks came in real thick. They're tough. You can't pull the feathers out. You practically have to use a pliers. They have a good taste to

**Setting out decoys. As every gunner knows, in predawn
darkness the decoys appear a lot farther from
the blind than they do when the sun finally rises.**

them, but you have to skin them, usually. By the time you pluck a ruddy duck, your fingers are plenty sore.

I like hunting with a companion. I don't like to go alone. I'm getting too old for that, now. You never know what could happen. I always like to hunt with somebody. It's more enjoyable. You sit there and have your sandwiches and coffee. It's cozy. One day last year, my hunting companion Ted Thyrion and I sat on a lake and it rained, rained, and rained.

We sat there until two o'clock. I had the boat canvas up to my lap. And I had my rain hood on. I didn't get wet. We got a few ducks—three mallard, a couple of bluebill, a couple of mudhen.

The cattails on Peats Lake are gone, along with most of the wild celery and other duck foods. There's still a few guys that hunt there. Even into the early 1970s, as you know, you could leave your skiff there, filled with your decoys, all through the hunting season, just like you could leave the door of your house unlocked. But no more. Most of the guys now hunt the fields for geese and mallard. You can hunt anywhere on Little Tail Point and Peats Lake, now. Grassy Island is gone.

Hank Bredael, who owned sporting-goods stores in Green Bay, died five or six years ago. He was very active in the Green Bay Duck Hunters Association.

The Green Bay Duck Hunters Association is still around. I'm on the Board of Directors. We meet two times a month.

All the duck shacks on the west shore of the bay were destroyed several years ago in a strong northeast storm.

We got one of the last shacks, though, and moved it to the Green Bay Sanctuary. It belonged to the Canoe and Duck Club. Now it holds two duck skiffs, old Green Bay decoys, a pulley that was used to draw the skiffs in from the bay to the inside of the shack, old hip boots, and other hunting gear. The shacks used to contain this stuff plus a stove and bunks. I remember going out to a shack and sleeping there on the night before opening day.

Yes, I'll be out on opening day this fall. I've never missed an opening.

Ted Thyrion's Story

I was born in Green Bay in 1911, and I was 13 years old when I began hunting. When I turned 14, I left eighth grade and worked with my brother-in-law out of Suamico on Green Bay as a commercial fisherman.

We'd get thousands and thousands of crayfish. We'd lift three hundred to four hundred boxes on set lines. We'd set a box every 25 feet, 50 to 60 boxes on a line, like a string of peas. There was a float attached to each end of the line, and a big stone was used for an anchor weight. We sold the crabs to Wisconsin Fishing. They'd boil them and sell them to taverns, where they'd be served in ice-cream cups.

Back then, you'd bring up a net and it'd be covered with pea-sized, black, freshwater snails. The wild ducks loved to eat them. There were so many that they'd cover the bottom of the boat, ankle-deep. There were millions of them, but they started disappearing in the 1930s. They were depleted by 1939 or 1940.

The cause, of course, was pollution. Pollution reduced the available lime in the water. The snails need lime for their shells. When the lime went, the snails went, too.

We tried to reestablish lime in certain areas but never were successful. Now, zebra mussels are appearing. They're a foreign exotic, but the ducks feed on them, so perhaps there's something to be said for the zebra mussel.

The river's cleaner, now, since the Clean Water Act. However, many marshes were damaged too badly, and others were filled in by highway construction and other landfill schemes. Peats Lake was damaged from fly ash blowing in from the power-plant dump that filled in Atkinson Marsh. The plant was built in the 1930s, and that's when everything began to worsen. That's when vegetation, duck food, and the ducks themselves began to decline on the bay.

Then, in 1973, a major storm washed out much of the west shore marsh on the bay. The marsh still hasn't recovered.

Reflections of cattails on a too-calm day on Green Bay. Unless the wind picks up, this outing may be remembered more for scenery than for flights of ducks.

Until the early 1940s, I generally hunted the bay, on Peats Lake and near the Town Line Road. But then I began to hunt the Fox River, too, near the mouth, where it empties into the bay.

I would hunt from the Yacht Club upriver to the first bridge that opened, the Green Bay and Western Railroad Bridge. I'd hunt the river, depending on the wind. The best wind was northeast. With a stormy northeast wind, the bay would be choppy and too rough for skiffs. The ducks would seek the sheltered river. The river had plenty of duck food during those years, too, all up and down the river.

I've made my own decoys, a couple hundred of them during my life. I made bluebill, bufflehead, teal, and canvasback.

My cousin, George Thirion, hunted on the river below the Lost Dauphin area and near the Nicolet Paper Company in De Pere. There was a nice slough near there.

We'd hunt the river with the number of decoys that a skiff would carry—about 30 to 35. The wooden birds weighed a lot. You needed a skiff to hunt the river because if you brought a duck down away from shore, the river was too deep to wade.

I had one good shoot for bluebill on a windy day on the river. A big tanker ship was coming downriver and passing by closely, as close as the length of a city block, about five hundred feet. Those bluebill flew in to the decoys right between us and that big ship. And we peppered the bluebill. We knew the shot wouldn't hurt that ship.

I had another big shoot in 1939 or 1940 on the inside of Long Tail Point. A cold front came down from Canada, bringing in the bluebill with it. There were four of us: Red Mahn, Wally Bentimer, Art "Skeig" Smith, and myself. The first day we got 187 bluebill. The next day we shot 80 or 90. And the third day we got a good number, too.

There are four major flights that come through on the river and bay. From mid-September (years ago, the season used to open that early) through early October is the first flight of teal, mudhen, and mallard.

The second flight, during the third week of October, is made up of fall bluebill (lesser scaup), big blue mudhen from Canada, shovellers, wigeon, gray ducks (gadwall), pintail, and redhead. This third week of October is always the best. This is the week that we'd take off from work.

Scaup by Milt Geyer.

The third flight, in early November, is the big bay bluebill (greater scaup), the northern mallard, and canvasback.

Then, finally, toward the final freeze, the cold-weather birds arrive: fish ducks (merganser), swans, whistlers (goldeneye), and butterballs (bufflehead).

I'd average out about 30 ducks a year during the good years. Remember, we couldn't get out every day. We all had full-time jobs.

I spent a lot of time on the water. From 1937 to 1951, I worked with Waterways Engineering, piloting and dredging. After that time, I worked at Fort Howard Paper Mill, from 1950 to 1976.

I met Milt Geyer on the marshes, and since 1975, when we both retired from work, we've been hunting together a lot. We go to places that have good duck food because, of course, that's where the ducks are.

These days, we put our skiffs on the trailer and just take off. We don't hunt from permanent blinds. We hunt from the skiffs. A blind sticks out and the ducks can see you. Our skiffs, though, slide right into the cattails. We're low and well hidden. We're a lot warmer in the skiffs than we'd be in a blind, too. We cover ourselves. Years ago, we'd use canvas tarps pulled up to our shoulders. Now, we use semiplastic covers. It's cozy.

We bring a radio along and set it in one of our gun boxes. Other stuff in our gun boxes includes compasses, hand warmers, first-aid kits, toilet paper, duck calls, shotgun shells, binoculars, matches, waterproof tape, and small tools.

Now, these days, it's like going on a picnic when we hunt. Milt and I have learned something over 40 years.

Working from a photo, Milt Geyer painted this rendition of his friend, Jack Schmitz,
poling through a marsh at Suamico on the bay's west shore to retrieve a drake mallard.

Milt Geyer with his redhead and bluebill decoys. Note the brown pad, used for comfort, on the bottom of the duck skiff.

Mallards by Milt Geyer.

New signs this afternoon
feathers floating on the wash
duck tracks in mud—
the flight's in from Canada

{ **Late October Visit** }

—*Stephen Miller*

Shotgun in one hand
burlap sack of ducks
slung over his shoulder
the heavy dead weight
of Depression years

{ **1931** }

—*Stephen Miller*

2

THe RIVeR

Bob Wurdinger's Story

I began duck hunting in 1927, when I was 15 years old. Throughout those years, I've hunted on the Fox River, though I also hunted on Lake Poygan and at Partridge Lake at Fremont. During the early season, there were lots of teal and mallard. With colder weather came the bluebill. We used wooden blocks, no plastics.

Back then, the season opened September 16 and closed on December 20. Toward the end of the season we shot bufflehead and goldeneye. We used bluebill decoys late in the season and included a few goldeneye. The goldeneye would land and then leave quickly. They're cautious. You shoot, and they dive right down and come out of the water flying. They're mostly in small flocks of three to four birds, sometimes as many as ten in a flock.

Bluebill are my favorite. They're dumb. You can stand up in a duck blind if you stand still. They come right in. Once they land in the decoys, you can shoot to beat hell. Sometimes they'll leave the decoys, circle, and come right back in.

We used wooden skiffs and patented oarlocks that allow you to row while facing forward. These oarlocks were the best. When a crippled duck dives, you want to go in that direction as fast as you can.

On the Fox River, one of the best blinds was on the brickyard point. Albert Ludke would hunt that point and generally be through hunting by 7:30 in the morning. In those days, 50 decoys per blind was the limit that you could set out. Years ago, there were blinds on every point of the river. There was a time when plugs were not required for guns. Albert Ludke had an extension on his gun and could put nine shells in.

When bluebill come, they're generally passing through. They only occasionally stay on the river to rest overnight.

At one time, canvasback were as common as mallard. There were 50 to 75 in a flock. The bluebill flocks also contained, generally, 50 to 75 birds.

Mallard over the Thousand Islands, Kaukauna, on the Fox River, on their way above the bluffs and toward cornfields for a couple of hours of feeding.

The back of Bob Wurdinger's blind on the river, north of Kaukauna. Inside, on the ceiling, are carefully cut strips of cardboard, which act as baffles to deflect the wind's force.

When I began hunting, the duck limit was fifteen, then it went to ten, then seven, then gradually to the point system. The most exciting hunts on the Fox River are often from the 10th to the 15th of November. The little bluebill come first, then, later, the big bluebill. For the past several years we have seen neither canvasback nor redhead.

I bought my decoys from Bill Steffen in 1929, and I painted them myself.

I set my decoys out, when hunting the river, 25 yards at the most from my blind. A lot of them are set in as close as 30 feet, to avoid cripples.

I set a clump of decoys on the right side of the blind and a second clump on the left. I leave an open space in front of the blind. The bluebill land at the head of the rig and then drift down to the opening. And they bunch up when they sense that something is wrong. That's the time to pepper them.

Across the river from my blind is the brickyard point. That's where, in 1929 or 1930, a flock of one hundred canvasback came in and all the birds in the flock were taken. There were 10 to 12 guys in the blind, and some of them had magazine extensions that were as long as their shotgun barrels.

Beginning in 1932, I worked for 11 years as a riverboat pilot on the Fox. I worked on the tugs because there were no other jobs, then. I first got on a boat when I was 16 or 17 years old. I knew quite a bit about the river before I signed on.

Going up and down the river in the autumn in those years you'd see lots of flights of bluebill and canvasback. You'd go past blinds with big rigs of decoys in front of them, rigs of 50 to 75 decoys. There were decoys all up and down the river.

I worked out of Kaukauna for Fox River Navigation. We had seven barges and two tugs, named the *Jane* and the *Ryan*. Often, we'd carry coal from Green Bay to the paper mills up the river. Each barge hauled an average of four hundred tons. We'd take empty barges down to Green Bay and return with full ones. We ran 24 hours a day, working two 12-hour shifts. Travel time from Green Bay to Kaukauna was 11 ½ hours.

I was a wheelman. We'd travel both day and night. I preferred to wheel at night. The darker it was, the better. You could see better, the darker it was. It was better to have all the lights turned off.

Inside a four-person Fox River blind. When a hunt is on, the curtain is drawn shut to ensure that the faces of the hunters are kept out of the sight of ducks and geese.

An October morning on the river. Water quality has improved over recent decades due to cooperation between mills and the Wisconsin Department of Natural Resources.

Fall was the most dangerous time. Rain would freeze, and a lock runner would jump from the back of a lock to get a line onshore to snub a barge down. The lock runner would have to get close to the front gate. Sometimes he'd slip. Once, when the *Ryan* was at the Little Chute lock, the lock runner jumped from the barge onto the back end of the lock wall. He slipped and fell in and drowned.

The river's wide between Green Bay and De Pere. We got wind-bound there a couple of times. Water would splash over the barge and over the coal.

The river is also wide from De Pere to Little Rapids. The Fox averages about six feet deep, but below De Pere there's more than 30 feet of water. The big lake steamers used to come up from Lake Michigan and the bay to the lower part of the river, to the Wells Dock. The steamers hauled pulpwood to Wells, and from there on our barges would pick up the cargo and go upriver.

From Kimberly to Appleton, the river is narrow, shallow, and rocky.

The river was no cleaner back then. It was dirtier. Everything was dumped into it. The mills polluted the river right and left. A lot of times the river smelled like pulp. The mills would dump, and dead fish would float downstream. There were pike and northerns to be caught, but they tasted bad.

I quit during the war. They wouldn't give me a raise. I was getting $114 a month, so I had to move on to working in the mill. Then the barges and tugs were sold because coal hauling on the river became less and less. Trucks began to move more of the cargo.

On the river, you always want to make your blind on a point. Upstream from me, some hunters near Ben Hoersch made their blind in the inlet. They didn't get ducks. They should have made their blind on the point.

I think that the prettiest part of the river is the lower part, from the Kaukauna Fifth Lock—where I've hunted ducks for so many years—to the De Pere bridge.

The flyway has changed. At the Rapide Croche Dam, most of the ducks cross the land. They don't cross over the river anymore. I've always hunted on the Fox River. When I hunted Lake Poygan, it wasn't good for hunting with decoys. There were too many other hunters out and about.

I like to cook bluebill. I parboil them first with onions and carrots. Then I rinse them, wipe and clean them well, and stuff them. The stuffing is made from bluebill parts and gizzard, plus hamburger, ground pork, celery, onion, poultry seasoning, and an egg and bread croutons mixed in. Mix the ingredients together real good. Bake at 350 degrees for a couple of hours, checking often to see when it's well-done. And while your bluebill are in the oven, baste them now and then with drippings.

Sometimes my wife, Rita, and I would go out to Lake Poygan in a boat blind, towing a skiff. We'd go out at 11 o'clock at night and sleep in the boat blind on a small mattress. "I slept good under the stars," says Rita. In the morning, we'd both shoot ducks.

Rita and I often went sturgeon spearing through the ice on Lake Winnebago, too. Rita got a 96 pounder, once. I've got sturgeon that were 80 pounds and 76 pounds.

Up until the past two years, we often got two hundred birds from my blind, for a season. We generally hunt until late morn-

Fair weather not for fowl. Morning's mist has lifted, the water is calm, and up and down the Fox River hunters are debating whether or not to bring in the decoys and call it quits.

A point blind on the Fox River. The right to hunt on favored points is often determined by customs that thread back through several generations of local hunters. It pays to ask, first.

A flock of wise mallard wheel into one of many sanctuaries along the bay and river.

Bob Wurdinger in his Fox River blind in 1985, on a crisp late-October morning.

ing. It's a four-man blind. A lot of times there would be only three of us hunting.

You asked me to describe one of my best hunts. It was around the 15 of November. One flock after the other set in. There were 40 to 50 bluebill in each flock. At one time, I had two hundred in the decoys, all bluebill. I couldn't load my gun fast enough. I was all alone in the blind.

Was that 40 or 50 years ago? No, that shoot took place six years ago.

{ Time Is Still }

Inside Bob Wurdinger's blind, downriver from The Thousand Islands,
Bob talks about my father, Marv, and my Uncle Glen at high school
track meets. "They'd be out running almost before the starting gun.
They time it just right so the starter can't call them back."

In the dark of the blind, the 1920s seem as fresh and close as
green willows hiding us. Time compresses. Bob stiffens.
Ducks are landing. He hears them splash in the decoys.

—*Stephen Miller*

The best duck hunting comes with a front moving in. A river blind
is dark and warm, especially if it's older and in good repair.

{ The Blind }

There's a small coal heater inside, or a propane burner
throwing warmth on hands raw from setting out four dozen decoys.

In all seasons the blind is sacred. It blends with the terrain.
It's located near a flight path or beside wild celery. In spring
and early summer, mallards use it for a nest site. On July
afternoons, you visit it with a girl. On mosquito-hazed
August evenings, you sit in its darkness,
calling brown-bellied ducks, which swing closer, closer.
In September, it's a hammering of nails
to secure willow branches, fresh tar paper.

The blind is dim light, stillness. Up and down the river scores of
churches hold satin green, red, and purple vestments within the
Sacristy. In the blind, these colors descend daily from heaven.

—*Stephen Miller*

Wally Mooney's Story

I was born in 1914. My first duck hunt was on opening day, September 16, 1929, on the Thousand Island area on the Fox River just outside of Kaukauna. There were thousands of ducks in this small area.

There were a couple hundred hunters, perhaps five hundred, on the Thousand Islands, behind every blade of grass it seemed. To the east was Red Bank Hill and to the south was Pine Woods Hill. There were 50 to 60 hunters on each hill. Ducks would come from the north, following the river, and hop these hills on their way to Lake Winnebago.

Shooting began at 5:30. I didn't shoot, but I was with my future brother-in-law, Bill Steffen. We were settled in a blind with decoys rigged out. Already, before shooting time, there were ducks in the decoys. Harold Engerson, the police chief, came slogging along the shoreline. "Slosh, slosh, slosh." He said, "Is anyone in the blind?" All the ducks in our decoys flew off. Even so, we were home by 6:45 that morning with 13 ducks.

Then, we went back in the afternoon. There was such a volley of gunfire that morning. I spent the afternoon with my head down, reloading guns for Billy Steffen and the other gunners.

On October 12 of that year, I was on Red Bank Hill, shooting ducks as they came over. I got four to five bluebill. This was a year of big flights.

It was that year that 212 canvasback were bagged in one morning from the brickyard blind, located on the river north of the Thousand Islands. That year the blind was built to hold 10 to 12 men. The foremen of Thilmany Paper Mill were hunting from there that morning. They brought in the 212 canvasback to the waxing room at the mill and had the workers remove the feathers from the birds and clean them.

The brickyard point blind back then had a clubhouse nearby, where you could drink coffee and then sneak down to the blind when a flock landed. One morning Al Klammer was in the blind alone. More than two hundred ducks landed in the

Wally Mooney, Kaukauna waterfowl hunter, decoy carver, and naturalist. Wally's hunting experiences on the Fox River began in 1929.

A misty morning on the banks of the Fox, when nocturnal raccoons and owls are returning
to their dens, and day creatures—deer and pheasant—are just beginning to stir.

On the Fox River, a half-dozen diving duck decoys made by Kaukauna
carver and hunter Jerome Kilgas and puddle ducks made by Steve Miller.

One way to lose altitude quickly is to perform the maneuver known as side-slipping. Some geese, when executing this move, actually turn completely upside down.

decoys. He had two guns in the blind. He began shooting and didn't get a single bird.

In the year of 1929, you could stand on one of the hills near Thousand Islands from daylight until eight or nine o'clock and there would always be flocks of migrating ducks in sight.

The last of the big flocks was in the 1940s. I hunted ducks

from 1929 through 1945, and in 1947. I quit until 1950, and then I hunted from 1950 through 1960.

I remember the Armistice Day Storm of 1940. I was on Lake Butte des Morts. That day, we went out in a big flat-bottom boat and set out only 18 decoys. The fellow who owned the blind arrived and asked us to leave. Because of the

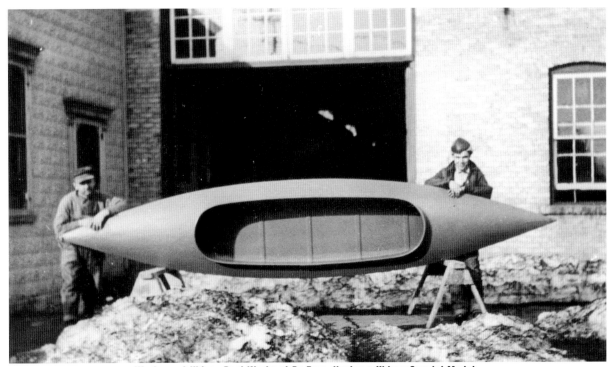
Workers at Kidney Boat Works at De Pere display a Kidney Special Model.

wind, it took us 45 minutes to pick up those 18 decoys. We didn't realize how bad the weather was until that noon, back in Kaukauna, I tried to walk across the Lawe Street bridge and the wind almost blew me off my feet.

The flocks were bigger years ago, of course, than they are now. A small flock would be made up of 15 to 25 ducks. A big flock would be in the hundreds of birds. Redhead and canvas-back were common, and they would often fly together in a single flock.

When I hunted alone, I would use 20 to 25 decoys. In the 1950s, hunting with Chuck Egan at the brickyard, we would set out 75. We would paint our decoys dark for the first of the season, and about mid-November we would paint many of the birds whiter, for goldeneye shooting.

When hunting goldeneye, we would push a skiff across the ice to a hole, pushing with a 16-foot pike pole. We would set out five to six decoys, lie down in the boat, and pull a white sheet over us. We'd let the goldeneye set. We'd shoot one. Then the flock would dive. When the flock surfaced again, each bird would take off in a different direction. It was better than skeet shooting. We'd push the skiff into the ice hole, retrieve the ducks, then pull the skiff back onto the ice with the pike pole.

Once, I tipped over in the skiff when it was four below zero. Walking home, the legs of my pants were like stovepipes. I came down with pneumonia a week later.

Most of the skiffs back then were Dan Kidney boats, made downriver in De Pere. Face-forward oarlocks were very popular, and a few of the old-timers still have them. They were great for chasing a limpy, but some of us were almost as quick, while facing forward, using regular oarlocks.

Other hunters from that era include Bob Goetzman and Bob Wurdinger.

One of the most interesting shooters was Bill Steffen. He was left-handed. Bill had a 10-gauge, lever-action shotgun. In the early days, you could use seven shells. As a flock would pass by in front of the blind, he would begin with the gun on his one shoulder and then move it over to his other shoulder, depending on which way the ducks were passing.

Back in 1929, the duck season ran late, 96 days. It ended on December 20.

Morning on the river. Standing beside a blind brushed in with willow
branches, a hunter considers prevailing winds and how to place the decoys.

Willow thickets, cottontails, pheasants on the east shore.
You walk out of town, hunt, return at midday to the De Pere bridge.

{ **Armistice Day, 1955** }

Men slip a wreath over the railing. Rifles fire.
The flowers are garish, floating on black water rolling
between banks of new snow, near cattails in velvet,
stalks fading into mute brown and canvas.

—Stephen Miller

**Mallard bask in sunshine within the protected borders of Thousand Islands
Environmental Center, Kaukauna, near a tree where eagles nest and raise their young.**

The East De Pere High School football practice field sits on a bluff above the Fox River and it's here where you, in late afternoon, run, tackle, catch passes, block, do squats and sit-ups. Then you stand and watch flocks sweeping upriver from the bay, the dark silent shape of ducks against gray sky. The birds pass above the bridge, set their wings, and glide lower, lower. A pause. Then, the sound of shotguns, muffled echoing from a point of fiery maples and nearby, coach's voice: You! Get back here!

— Stephen Miller

{ **The Agonies** }

A blind on the shore of the Fox River, near Kaukauna. Standard
equipment includes a boat, several dozen duck and goose
decoys, binoculars, lunch, and a large serving of patience.

Jerome Kilgas' Story

I was born in Kaukauna in 1911. I began duck hunting at age 17. Before that I would help out at the blinds on the Fox River, setting out decoys and pulling them out, helping the older gunners. I think they liked me being out with them because I'd do errands for them.

This all took place at Kaukauna's Thousand Islands and just downriver from Thilmany Paper Mill. The most common ducks were bluebill, mallard, whistler. Pintail were common then, too.

Most of the decoys used were made in the early 1920s and 1930s. I hunted a lot near the brickyard. We'd set out one hundred decoys sometimes. We set the decoys out four feet apart from each other. All the different species we mixed together. And it's not necessary to have all the decoys facing in the same direction, either.

We set the decoys out in two groups. An open space was left in the middle, in front of the blind.

I began making decoys in 1934. I'm still making them. I estimate that over the years I've carved at least a couple hundred. The first were a couple of pieces of wood that I nailed together. I wish I still had them.

The decoys can be painted any color, but the blackish-colored ones bring in the ducks best. They show up well on the water.

I used to hunt with Bill Steffen, another decoy maker from Kaukauna. He was a skilled hunter. He also had great success at finding Indian artifacts such as arrowheads and chipping stones in the hills around the river.

One year someone stole all my decoys from my blind, about 45 decoys in all. They were mostly wooden ducks which I'd carved plus nine goose decoys made from cork by August Sosnoski. They shot out the bottom of my aluminum boat, too. There was no way to repair it. Why would anyone want to do a thing like that? I don't know. You know, if they would have said,

Setting out wooden bluebill and black-duck decoys on the Fox River.

"I'd like a couple of decoys," I'd said, "Take them." But don't do damage to them. For heaven's sake.

We never locked the blind. There was no sense to it. Were they trying to get me off the point? I don't know. I never hurt anybody. If they'd wanted to hunt with me, hell, I had a lot of room there. Vic Gerhartz and I hunted together. We got along good. What I wanted to do, he wanted to do.

About 15 years ago another rig of my decoys was stolen from the roof of my garage. I had put them up there to dry the paint, to help take the shine off. Someone later knocked at my door and said, "Here's an envelope I found near your mailbox." I don't remember what he looked like.

Inside was $50 and a note. "I stole some of your decoys. If I'm forgiven, put the words 'I'm forgiven' on the envelope and put the envelope inside the vestibule of St. Mary's Church."

Did I ever tell you about the seagulls?

One day, Harold Engerson, who was police chief of Kaukauna, took a fellow hunting who had a heavy accent and who recently came over from the Old Country. This was the guy's first hunting trip, and he felt it was a big deal to be going out with the police chief.

Three seagulls flew over the blind, low. "Shoot! Shoot! Shoot!" said Harold. The guy up and shot two.

He took them home and cooked them. They smelled up his kitchen so bad. The guy never went duck hunting again.

I used to hunt from the beginning to the end of the duck season. In cold weather, you'd shiver and your teeth would rattle and you'd stay there. Everybody said we were crazy. Some of them weren't joking.

We'd hunt at least three days a week. You'd get down to the blind at four o'clock, three-thirty in the morning, and put your decoys out. When daybreak came along, it was well paid for. Then there were ducks, so many ducks! Mostly all bluebill. So many bluebill! And whistler.

Our decoys never all looked the same. They were all different species and we set them out facing in different directions.

We'd take one thousand ducks a year or better from our blind. You'd come back with a gunnysack half full.

Or two sacks half full.

Way back then when we worked in the mill, there were times that you did not even have to punch out to go duck hunting. You just went.

A Jerome Kilgas diving-duck decoy and two black ducks await company from higher up.

Once we got a bunch of about 15 ducks for the top guys at the mill who were going to have a big game feed for important people coming from out of town. We put the ducks in the waxer in the mill, like we always did. You get the wax over the feathers and the feathers come off slick when you peel the wax off after it's cooled.

Well, this time there was a problem at the other end of the mill. We all ran up there. We forgot about the ducks in the waxer.

When we got back, we lifted those ducks out. Well, just the feet and the legs came up. The ducks had been in the waxer so long, they'd cooked!

There was no wild game dinner that night!

Early in the morning on the river it used to be one flock after another, all flying south. Bing. Bing. Bing. Bing. One flock would disappear and another would be coming up the river.

The other river hunters? There was Speedy Mitchell, Van Eyk, and Pleshek. They were in another crowd at the mill. Bert Roberts hunted with Pleshek. Pleshek's decoys were old and were certainly made before the 1920s. They go back to the 1800s.

Wally Mooney and I never hunted together. But we used to work together in the mill. Wally was my damper man.

I could never stick to a job and hold it down. I'd get promoted as high as I could go. Then I'd ask to be switched to another operation in the mill, where I'd start at the bottom again and work my way toward the top.

I don't hunt the river anymore. The hill on the way down to the blind is very steep. One morning in the dark on my way down I fell into a gully that hadn't been there before.

I was a loner about all my life. I still go hunting alone and I shouldn't. But if I can sneak away and go hunting I'm in my seventh heaven.

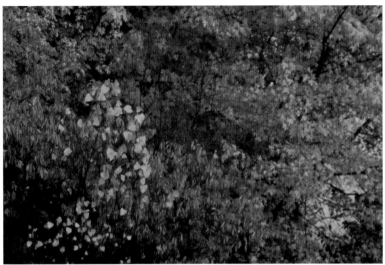

Bursting forth in full colors, October's woodlands are only weeks away from being stripped down to black, wet branches, bent under the weight of first snow.

Lowry Wurdinger, October 1994, standing beside his Fox River blind, which is camouflaged with willow cuttings. Earlier in the day, two Canada geese were shot here.

A flock of geese over a secluded part of the river in October.

At the sink.

Earl Loyster's Story

Earl Loyster hunted the upper waters of the Fox River from the 1930s through the early 1980s. The river, near Montello and Portage, is narrow in parts. One can almost jump from one bank to the other. It widens as it nears Oshkosh and Lake Winnebago. The flyways of the upper Fox include the famed hunting areas of Lake Puckaway, Grand River Marsh, Lake Maria, Buffalo Lake, Lake Butte des Morts, Lake Winneconne, Lake Poygan, and Little Lake Butte des Morts.

I was born in 1912. After high school, I applied for work at the Milwaukee Public Museum and found myself working with Owen Gromme, the famous naturalist and bird artist. I was the chief collector for the Bird Department between 1930 and 1935. In 1929, Owen taught me how to use a gun and how to hunt. In fact, on one of our first outings, collecting specimens for the museum, Owen was walking on the bank of a ditch when my gun went off, blowing a chunk of dirt out from under Owen's feet. The only thing Owen said was, "Earl, be more careful."

In the 1930s, I was on the duck marshes just about every month of the year, collecting birds in varied seasonal plumage for the museum. For months, I stayed on Lake Maria in Green Lake County. I had a trailer that the museum owned. It was the first steel trailer made, a Hayes trailer. Gromme had gone to the Chicago Automobile Show and had seen them there. When he got back to Milwaukee, he bought it through the museum. He got a very good price on it, about $8,000. It sold for around $12,000 at the time. Well, on Lake Maria, I had two bird skinners, a cook, and myself. We all lived there. We had a big wall tent with a floor, where we kept our excess sleeping bags. I had a list of about 20 birds that they wanted for the systematic collection. I went down to the lake every day. The museum banded ducks there, also.

During the Armistice Day storm of November 11, 1940, when many hunters had close calls and some died, I almost didn't make it back myself. I was hunting on Lake Maria. I was dressed lightly. The temperature was close to 60 degrees that morning. But it fell by 40 degrees in a matter of hours. The wind was so strong that my blind blew away from around me. The water turned to slush. You couldn't walk on it and you couldn't paddle through it. I left my decoys, lay down in my skiff, and the wind blew me in to shore. You couldn't even walk, the wind was so strong. I crawled up a hill through a blizzard, to a farmyard. I was exhausted. I couldn't move farther. And I was being covered with snow. Then, a gust blew the metal roof off of a shed. It made so much noise that the farmer, Ernest Weber, came out of his house to look. Every time he looked my way, I'd shout. Once, he looked my way and I rolled my body sideways. Finally, he saw me and pulled me into the house.

You ask about the decoys that I lost that day. There were 18 or 19, a rig I'd made at the museum. There were three mallard, two pintail, and I think a baldpate in there, too. Those were the puddle ducks I had. I also had 13 mixed bluebill and ringneck. Each decoy had its own canvas sack. Each sack had a strong cord, so you could carry the sacks with decoys in them over the barrel of your shotgun.

For anchor cords, I used rope that's sold to raise and lower wooden windows. I dyed the rope to match the vegetation of the marshes.

They made a nice stool, those birds. You know, the funny thing was, the day after the storm I tried to go out and get them, but I couldn't. I kept falling through. The ice was thick, but it was just like the ice on the edge of your refrigerator. Just spongy. It looked like Styrofoam. It would let you right down. It froze so fast that it had a lot of air in it. That's why they had so much trouble rescuing people. No helicopters, then. All they could do was break out to the hunters who needed rescuing.

But back to the decoys. They were about two hundred yards out, on a point. When I came back about two weeks later, when the ice had firmed up, I could see where each one of them had been chopped out. I don't think they were labeled at all. They might have had my initials on them, but that's all.

Owen Gromme called me up one day to tell me he was going to visit his brother-in-law. He said, "I'd like to go up to

The Fox River's Thousand Islands area at Kaukauna, a hunting center since 12,000–8,000 B.C.,
as evidenced by archaeological artifacts collected here by Mrs. William Steffen from 1915 to 1942.

Earl Loyster with a drake mallard on a Fox River marsh, November 12, 1974.

Lake Maria with you this weekend." So we drove up to his brother-in-law's place. I think it was Lake Mason at Briggsville. We stayed overnight, and his wife went along with their setter dog.

Early in the morning, we dropped down to Lake Maria. It was frozen solid. But sitting in the ice, out in the middle, were a lot of ducks. Sitting on the ice, you know? "Well," said Gromme, "I'm going to try something." So he went to town and bought a bottle of laundry bluing. He mixed it in a five-gallon bucket and sloshed it out onto the ice where we were going to hunt.

Some of the birds were working around the frozen lake. We set out about 20 decoys on the ice, and I guess we were there about 20 minutes. A big old mallard came wheeling around. It was a black mallard. It went just past our blind and sat down on the ice and walked into the cattails. I thought I could jump that bird and shoot it. Gromme told me to go ahead. So I walked down shore and was well within gun range of the bird. I was wondering why he didn't fly away. I almost walked right on top of him before he flew up. Whoom. Down he came. So I started to walk out on the ice to get the bird, and I turned around to look at the blind. There were 160 bluebill just sitting

on that fake water. I saw Gromme stand up in the blind and the ducks were in the air. I could see the smoke come out of Gromme's gun from the shot, and the ducks were just dropping. He killed 23 of them out of that flock. They were wadded up so tight that every shot took eight or nine birds. We were through hunting. We had our limit of ducks.

I learned a lot from Gromme about hunting ducks. He had an old rattletrap 12-gauge. When you shook it, it rattled like a bucket of bolts. He would pull the trigger and down went the first duck. He'd hold the trigger down and keep pumping. The gun would shoot every time another shell pumped into the chamber.

He was so good at shooting. Not only did he shoot ducks as a boy and growing up, he also had opportunities because he had friends that had excellent duck hunting places. Ed Ahern had some of the best places that I have ever been in. One was on Lake Winnebago, at Long Point.

At one place, Ahern had a tunnel that went from the duck shack, underground, to the end of the blind. So, you never had to expose yourself. All you had to do was crawl on your hands and knees on a carpet, underneath the ground.

Earl Loyster in the 1920s, with a catch of northern pike.

Lake Maria, Green Lake County, 1938, where Earl Loyster collected ducks for the
Milwaukee Public Museum collection, working under Owen Gromme. This is the lake
where Earl had his close call during the famous Armistice Day storm of 1940.

You'd set your gun outside the shack so it was the same temperature as the outside. You wouldn't have any temperature factor to worry about. That's one thing I learned from Gromme, that when it's cold, don't bring your gun inside and expect it to shoot when you go outside again.

Long Point is north of Fond du Lac. It was a long, narrow extension with bulrushes growing along one side of it. It tipped out into a beautiful stone blind, built out of local stone that was picked up along the shore. It had a seat in it, made out of railroad ties. Had a stove in it. There was a man who would take the decoys out and take them in. They put 78 decoys out. The first morning we hunted it, the guy had already set the decoys out. We all had a nice breakfast. Ahern and I sat there for maybe a half an hour. A hundred fifty or sixty bluebills swung in. We had five flocks, just like that, come right into the decoys. It was beautiful.

Ahern took Gromme and me to Eldorado Marsh, just north of Waupun. It was a real marshy land, which has long since been drained out. The state owns some of it and has a hunting ground there. The geese use it. But back then, Ahern had this shack, very comfortable, with bunk beds in it, with enough

room to sleep six. They had a blind built up in a partially wooded place with willows sticking up around the back. There was a big marsh around it. They had an American water spaniel, there. This is the funniest thing. It was cold that day, so we let the dog sit in the blind. The dog had fleas. So, it was thump-thump-thump. Thump-thump-thump. "Come here, you," said Ahern. "You're making too much noise. You're going back to the shack."

So the dog was taken back to the shack. Ahern's wife had made him a greenwing teal sandwich for lunch, and damned if the dog didn't eat it. Ahern was really mad at that dog.

We killed quite a few mallard, about 10 or 12. It was very good shooting. That evening, we built a good hot fire at the shack and put our feet up. The dog was sleeping. Every so often there was the thump-thump-thump. Thump-thump-thump. All of a sudden, the dog peeled off a fart that fairly raised the shingles. The dog jumped up, eyes wide open, legs stiff, and began growling and barking.

You ask about great shoots. Well, in the early 1930s, I was hunting Lake Poygan. Pages Slough is on the north side of the lake. It's a big marsh with a dredge ditch going north and south

Earl Loyster preparing for a fishing and camping outing, circa 1930.

**Earl Loyster, checking equipment before
departing to a Wisconsin lake in the 1920s.**

of the Wolf River. I had been hunting out of the Richter's Resort, which is on the east shore of the river. The resort catered to duck hunters. I had gone out to the point to a blind, what they call the Lone Point.

I watched all day long. About 100,000 ducks and geese went over me, very, very high, leaving the country. No shooting at all. About four o'clock in the afternoon, a mallard wheeled in from the lake, going against the wind. He was apparently going back to the marsh to spend the night. He was up there. Fifty, sixty yards. Something like that. I thought that this was the only shot I had all day. I'm going to take it! I led him about 10 feet, and he dropped like a "thump." He dropped way behind me because the wind had carried him. So I started to poke back in there, winding up near a tree on the shore. I kept walking and walking. Finally a voice said, "Your duck is over here."

A guy stood up from out of a blind. He said, "That was the best damn shot that I have seen anybody make in the past 10 years."

I told him that I was lucky, that the bird was up there pretty high. He said, "You bet he was up there high. I don't think I would have shot at him." His name was Montford. He worked at the Northwestern Mutual Life Insurance Company. He said that anyone who could shoot a duck like that, he'd like to hunt with him. I told him that the season was about over. He said, "Yeah, that's true. Those birds flying over are on their way to Texas."

The next year, I get a telephone call at the museum. It was this guy, Montford. He was up at Richter's Resort. He said that he had a beautiful day of hunting the day before and he didn't know why we couldn't have a couple more. He asked if I could make it up there. I told him I had to check with the boss. I turned around and talked to Gromme, and he said, "Sure. Go ahead. You have the time coming." This was on a Friday. It was November. I went home, packed up my gun, decoys, and the whole works. I got to Richter's about 11:30 that night. Six or seven guys were still around, slurping coffee and talking about what a wonderful hunt it was that day. I was tired so I went to bed.

I got up four a.m. Montford had a little square boat, wider at the back. It couldn't have been more than 12 feet long. It was wooden, about three feet wide, maybe three and a half or four. He had a little five-horse motor on the back. I sat between the decoys

Lake Maria, 1939. A member of Earl Loyster's research team, releasing banded baldpate as part of a Milwaukee Public Museum study.

in front of the little front seat, and he sat on the backseat. "Putt-putt-putt," off we went, about two miles into Pages Slough.

You wouldn't believe the mallard that were coming out. We headed toward a back area. He said, "I have a blind back here. Those ducks are all going to come back in here to feed. You mark my words." So I sat back, watching all these ducks going overhead. Some of them were in range.

Well, we got all set. We even had live decoys. They were four mallard in a case that sat on top of the wooden decoys. When we got the wood decoys set out, we put one live mallard in front of the blind. It quacked and quacked. Another live decoy that we set out with the wooden ones would call back. They called back and forth.

About 20 minutes after we set up, the first flock of about 15 came in. It was beautiful. They wanted to sit right in with the decoys. I had never seen anything like this. I said, "Now you tell me when you are going to shoot. I'll wait for you to shoot." He said, "When you see me raise my gun, you'll know then." That was a good way to do it.

Flocks of 20, 25, 30 mallard were coming in to us. You wouldn't believe that many ducks would flock in. We killed

our limits of mallard there.

Montford told me that if I wanted to stay over, a fellow by the name of Erdman was coming up the next day, a buddy who liked to hunt ducks. He was going to bring a double-ended duck skiff. You know, pointed at either end. We would then tow him behind Montford's boat and go up to Pages Slough again.

The following morning, it was frozen solid. There was at least an inch of ice. We had to break ice to get to the channel. Then Montford couldn't get the motor started. He poured a little gasoline on the carburetor to get it hot. He lit the gas. He kept the gas tank cap on the motor screwed on, of course. Then he put his gloves over the flames to put them out, pulled the line, and away we went.

We got into the channel of the Wolf River, started toward Pages Slough, and turned due north. When we got one hundred yards into Pages Slough we hit ice. We broke a sheet of ice about two feet long and it went right into the skiff. It was like putting a knife through it. We sank in three feet of water.

There we were. Decoys all over. Holding our guns and shells up. We tried to wade back to shore, then we waded back to get more stuff.

Montford looked at the skiff as we pulled it out of the water. He said, "I think I can fix that. Do you have a bandanna?" We all had one. After rolling them up, we tucked them into the crack that the ice had cut. It was a nice clean crack. The skiff's floor boards were about three-eighths of an inch thick. We took them out of the skiff, hammered them apart, saved the nails, then used decoy weights to nail the floorboards all the way around that crack.

After repairing the skiff, Montford said that we'd hunt right there. It was very cloudy at the time. It looked like a thunderstorm was brewing.

We had open water so we put our decoys out because we had a lot of them. Between the three of us, we must have had 50. We didn't take the mallard decoys, only bluebill. Here we are in our boots, lying down in the marsh. It was not hard marsh, but soft. A little water leaked into the boot area, with each movement causing more water to leak in. Then it started to snow, great big wet flakes about two inches across. It was hitting us on the back of our hats. We were completely prone.

All of a sudden there was a noise, just like a thunderstorm. A hundred and sixty-some ducks came in. All of them were over the decoys and then, whoosh, they were gone. We watched the flock split just before they disappeared in the snow. One bunch went north, and the other bunch flew down and sat right down in front of us. They were about 20 to 25 feet away. There was a strong wind blowing right into our faces. It was hard to hear the whispers going on between us.

Montford kept saying, "Don't shoot until I'm ready. Let's get organized. Earl, you take the left since you're on that side. I'll take the middle. And Erdman, you take the right." You wouldn't believe the numbers of ducks that fell out of that flock when we shot them. We shot nine shells and knocked down pretty close to 40 ducks. It took a half of an hour to kill the cripples. I got into the skiff and I paddled out into the mess of dead birds and started throwing them into the boat. Montford and Erdman said that I had them all, so I started back in. I broke my oar through some ice and pulled a bluebill right on top of the surface. He'd dove under the ice and died. These were all bluebill. They were beautiful. We had 42 ducks. We were shy three ducks for a full limit.

We loaded up the boats. I sat in the damaged skiff, which was towed. I sat in the back, with all the dead ducks, so that

The Milwaukee Public Museum banding and collecting station at Lake Maria, 1930. The trailer, made by Hayes Trailer Company, was the first U.S.-made steel trailer.

the bow would ride high, so that our repair job would be out of the water. It worked. We didn't ship any water. The wind was blowing. It was quite a pull back, against the wind. I was completely sheathed in ice when we got to Richter's landing. And the ducks were frozen together. But we got back.

You asked about the time we saw will-o'-the-wisp. This all started when a friend called me, wanting to go to Lake Poygan because he hunted up there, some. We started out of Milwaukee on a Friday afternoon. We got to Poygan about 11 or 11:30 or something like that. Straight out, we went out to this one blind that was way out on a point. If you didn't get there early and get into it, someone else would have it before you got there. Other hunters usually came in about two o'clock in the morning. We got there about midnight and cleared everything out of the blind and laid our sleeping bags down. This guy wanted to smoke a cigarette, so we stood there, talking to each other. I turned around and saw this purple ball. It flared up right out of the marsh, about one hundred yards behind us. I didn't know what the hell it was. Then it went flittering off under the fog, like sheet lightning.

It would then catch another pocket and go off into another sort of purple ball. Like an X-ray light. Neither one of us knew what it was. I had remembered that Gromme said something about methane gas, so I imagine that is what this was. It went on for quite a while, 15 or 20 minutes. We finally got tired of watching it. This guy was a little bit alarmed about it, but he said it wasn't coming anywhere near us, because we were out on the point and it seemed to be only over the marsh. I don't know what triggered it.

The air was very calm, and there was fog about head-high off the water. The fog wasn't as thick on the point as it was back in the marsh. The fog was five or six feet high, I think. It was very level. I finally figured that the purple balls must be methane gas that was collecting under the fog in pockets. It would just be ignited from pocket to pocket.

The fog wasn't over the water much, but over the marsh. Then there were little wisps of it over the lake, but not much. There was just a slight breeze blowing in the night, with the marsh part protected. The wind didn't take hold, so it just hung in the marsh pockets. I'm sure that if you talked with anyone who has lived around the marsh for a long time, they probably

Earl Loyster with a trophy whitetail taken in Oneida County in November of 1951.

The witchery of the Fox River marshlands.

have seen this. Gromme told me later, after I told him about it, that the Fond du Lac marsh used to have will-o'-the-wisps on it. He had seen it. And he said he'd read about it on Horicon Marsh. It occurs usually at night when you've got darkness and no light because I suppose that in the daylight you wouldn't see it much, if it was there. It makes sense that it would be at night, and it would be a contrasting color to darkness. I had never seen it before or since.

E

veryone in the De Pere barbershop seems to have a duck blind
near the tuberculosis sanatorium on the river where, if you look up
the hill, you can see the cabin of the lost dauphin staring darkly
with its broken windows. In October, fowl are scattered all over
the widespread, mallards, mudhen, bluebill, bobbing up and down
feeding on duck potato, duckweed, wild rice. The barber
tells what it's like a half hour before dawn on Saturday, the shoreline
packed with guys and a bunch of ducks coming upriver, dipping down,
everybody shooting, and a single bird fluttering down into the channel.
The hunters jump into their boats, pull starter cords on too cold outboards,
the three horsepowers choking into life, the race on. The air still filled
with dark from the night before. Hunters shooting at each other.
Shot rattles off the sides of cedar skiffs. A load of number 4s
whapping against the cattail sides of a blind. Inside the sanatorium,
patients stir, a spoon handle rattles against a cup, the windows blush
with sunrise, the glass panes muffling the roar of Remington Wingmasters.

— Stephen Miller

{ **Wingmasters** }

In the parking lot
of the Zig Zag Bar
{ **Hunter's Moon** }   overhead
yelping in fog
snow geese

—Stephen Miller

3

APPeNDIXES

Appendix A

Green Bay–Area
DeCOYS

WORKING DECOYS OF GREEN BAY AND THE LOWER FOX RIVER

Special thanks to the late Hank Braedel for help in providing background information on many of these decoys and their carvers. Thanks also to private owners of decoys and the Green Bay Duck Hunters Association, which maintains a collection on display at the Green Bay Sanctuary.

This is not a comprehensive catalog but a sampling of working decoys found in this small but diverse area.

Drake goldeneye by George La Plante, Green Bay, 1911.
La Plante was a commercial fisherman and market
hunter on the bay from the early 1900s to 1920.

Drake canvasback, 1906, by Axel J. Johnson. Johnson, a commercial
fisherman, had a cabin on Little Tail Point. He hunted both Little Tail
and Long Tail Points. His decoys were of a large size for open water.
He operated a fish house until his death.

Teal decoy from the hands of Louis Hutzler Sr., 1910. Hutzler
was in charge of the First Lighthouse on Green Bay for many
years and hunted both ducks and geese.

John Voletz decoy, 1900. Voletz did most of his
hunting on the east bay shore in Door County.

Pensaukee black ducks from the early 1900s. Decoy on right was made
by Ralph Johnson; decoy on left is by an unknown maker. Both were
used at the mouth of the Pensaukee River and on Charles Pond
on Little Point (one of the hottest shooting ponds in the area until
the 1920s). With high heads and good workmanship, these oversized
decoys were made to withstand heavy seas.

Bluebill by Ralph Sorquet, Green Bay, 1920.

Robert McAllister decoy, 1920, Green Bay. McAllister was a farm owner.

West shore hunting cabin, near Suamico.

Chet Barlament canvasback, 1929, Green Bay.

Duck shack, west bay shore, owned by decoy maker John Basteyns.

Close-up view of duck shack that Milt Geyer
moved, with the Corps of Engineers, from the west
shore of the bay to the Green Bay Sanctuary property.

Steve Miller on the Fox River south of De Pere in
1955 with his handmade black-duck profile decoys.

Lem C. Cross puddle duck, 1930. Little is
known about this Green Bay–area carver.

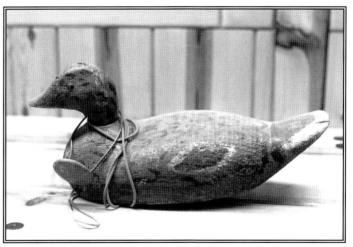

Lem C. Cross decoy, 1930.

Lem C. Cross decoy, 1930.

Lem C. Cross, cork-bodied canvasback, 1930.

Diving duck by Jack Francois. Many of his good-quality decoys
(1920–1940), made from cedar and cork, were for his own use and
for sons Norbert and Wesley. Francois was better known for his duck
boats, strip-built with long flaring bows, made from cedar and pine.
Good marsh boats, they also rode well in open water.

Drake canvasback decoy, cork, by Jack Francois.

Hollow drake bluebill decoy by Jack Van Kauwenberg of Green Bay,
1940s. According to Hank Braedel, Van Kauwenberg's major carving
years were 1930 through 1955, when he produced as many as one
thousand decoys per year (in standard and deluxe grades). All were
handmade and very uniform; about half were hollow.

Drake mallard by Jack Van Kauwenberg, 1933.
Van Kauwenberg also made violins and boats.

Bluebill by Ben Geyer (brother to Milt Geyer), 1938. Ben hunted the bay area for many years and owned a hunting shack along Green Bay's west shore. He also was a trapper.

Clarence Geyer bluebill, 1935. Another brother of Milt Geyer, Clarence hunted with Milt, often walking along the marsh, jump shooting for mallard. Clarence almost drowned in the bay, then he stopped duck hunting.

Redhead by Steve Delahout, 1942, Green Bay. Steve hunted geese in fields but also liked to hunt deer and ducks, according to Milt Geyer.

Milt Geyer black duck, 1937, with a head and body to be envied by any carver.

Coot by Joe Anderson, 1965, Green Bay. Joe is a son of Don Anderson.

Hen bufflehead by Bill Maricque, 1948. Maricque was a great canvasback hunter who ran a tavern in Green Bay.

Les Rondow diving duck, 1944, Green Bay. Les
"is a carver of everything," according to Milt Geyer.

Teal by Don Anderson, 1960. Anderson hunts waterfowl and
upland birds around the Naverino area, where he has a cottage.

Drake bufflehead by Ted J. Thyrion, 1973, Green Bay.
A close hunting companion of Milt Geyer's, Ted makes
canvasback decoys and repairs duck skiffs.

Crab trap made by Ted Thyrion. Ted would set out
hundreds of these traps on the bay in the 1940s.
He and Milt Geyer still use these traps, baited with
dead fish, when hunting or fishing the bay.

Cliff Walker bluebill, 1980, Green Bay, Peaks Lake area.

Ruddy duck drake by Don Datzman, 1975. Datzman
hunted most of the bay and made his own decoys.

Milt Geyer drake bluebill, 1992.

Milt Geyer hen bluebill, 1992.

Fox River
DeCOYS

Mallard from the hands of a carver named Pleshek, from
Kaukauna's south side, late 1800s through early 1900s.

Bluebill by Pleshek, 1800s or early 1900s.
Note nail head used to represent eyes.

Goldeneye by Pleshek.

A 1940s Ted Thyrion canvasback drake, hunted over for half a century on the Fox River and Green Bay, and a Thyrion-made crayfish trap.

Drake canvasback from Kaukauna, Fox River, circa early 1900s.

Goldeneye by unknown maker, Kaukauna, circa early 1900s.

Bill Steffen bluebill, Kaukauna, 1920.

Forest "Speedy" Mitchell goldeneye decoy, Kaukauna, 1920.
Bob Wurdinger likes to set three or four of Mitchell's
goldeneye off to one side of his main decoy rig late in
the season, when whistlers migrate up the river.

Van Eyck bluebill, Kaukauna, 1920.

Jerome Kilgas canvasback drake, Kaukauna, from the 1920s.

A rig of bluebill and one redhead from the hands of Jerome Kilgas, 1992. These decoys flash a lot of white on windy days, thus drawing ducks away from hunters using larger numbers of decoys.

Jerome Kilgas with his decoys.

**Robert Popp of De Pere made this black duck in the early 1970s.
A skilled pattern maker, he carved dozens of decoys including
mallard, teal, canvasback, and bluebill, offering customers
a choice of heads: carved wooden or custom-molded plastic.**

Mallard drake by Robert Popp, early 1970s.

Robert Popp mudhen (freshwater coot), 1970s.

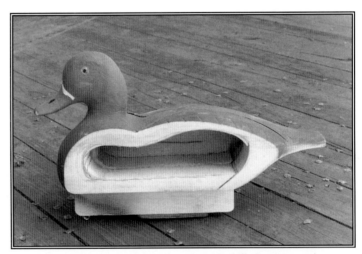

This cutaway of a Robert Popp hen bluebill shows an early attempt at constructing a hollow decoy with cedar boards fastened together vertically. Later, he adopted the conventional practice of fastening boards horizontally.

A Wally Mooney canvasback drake, Kaukauna, 1990.
Wally has been making decoys since 1929 when he
first hunted the Fox River with his then-future
brother-in-law, Bill Steffen, who also carved decoys.

A Wally Mooney goldeneye drake, Kaukauna, 1990.

A drake redbreasted merganser by Wally Mooney, 1990.

A hen redbreasted merganser by Wally Mooney, 1990.

An ad from a 1925 outdoors magazine. The finely crafted Kidney
wooden skiffs, built on the banks of the Fox River at De Pere,
still serve waterfowlers throughout the United States,
though the company ceased operation some decades ago.

Ted Thyrion and Milt Geyer, hunting pals and fellow conservationists,
in May of 1995 at Ted's home in Green Bay. Each spring and summer,
for many years, Ted and Milt rescued hundreds of stranded or
abandoned wild ducklings and brought them to safe refuges.

Milt Geyer black duck, 1963. Although it's a working decoy, feathers are carved, a typical feature of Milt's gunning birds.

A Fox River blind near Kaukauna in spring 1993. A hard winter has beaten down camouflage to reveal construction details.

Appendix B

FURTHER READINGS AND RESOURCES

BOOKS

American Waterfowl: Hunting Ducks and Geese by Bert Claflin. Alfred A. Knopf, New York. 1952. A classic duck hunting volume with important information about hunting the Fox River Valley marshes. The author was a Green Bay outdoors writer.

Decoys of the Winnebago Lakes by Ronald M. Koch. Rivermoor Publications, 5023 Rivermoor Drive, Omro, WI 54963. 1988. Wooden decoys from the central Fox River region.

Duck and Coot Ecology and Management in Wisconsin by Laurence R. Jahn and Richard A. Hunt. Technical Bulletin Number 33, Wisconsin Conservation Department, Madison, WI. 1964. A wealth of information about migration patterns and waters favored by waterfowl.

The Great Book of Wildfowl Decoys edited by Joe Engers. Thunder Bay Press, Inc., 5880 Oberlin Drive, Suite 400, San Diego, CA 92121. 1990. David Jon Spengler's chapter on Wisconsin decoys includes photos and documentation about carvings from the Green Bay and Fox River.

Stillers' Duck Camp: A Half Century of Waterfowling on Green Bay by Don Stiller. Alt Publishing Co., P.O. Box 400, Green Bay, WI 54305. 1994. A hands-on look at west shore fowling by a hunting guide and commercial fisherman with day-in, day-out hunting experiences over a time span of many decades. No one else comes close to Mr. Stiller's knowledge of how it's done.

PERIODICALS

"Armistice Day Nov. 11, 1940" by Tim Eisele, *Waterfowl Magazine*, December/January 1991. Tales from survivors of the great storm that trapped hunters throughout the Midwest.

"Rafting for Green Bay 'Bills,'" by Jack Hirt, *Wildfowl Magazine*, August/September 1999. Gunning for diving ducks on the bay's offshore waters.

"A Man's Got to Have His Priorities" by Mike Beno, *Ducks Unlimited*, January/February 1982. Accounts of hunting the waters of Green Bay and efforts to preserve the marshlands.

"Little Tail Journal" by Doug Ferdon, *Wisconsin Sportsman*, November/December 1986. Little Tail Point, on Green Bay's west shore, is a famous hunting site.

"The Midwest Classic" by Mike Beno, *Ducks Unlimited*, January/February 1983. A history of the Fox River's Dan Kidney and Son, builders of the famed duck skiffs.

Voyager: Northeast Wisconsin Historical Review. Articles on Dan Kidney Hunting Boats (Volume 4, Number 1, pp. 29–32) and duck hunting (Volume 8, Number 2, pp. 43–47).

Another extensive source of information is *A Bibliography on the History of Brown County Based on the collections of The State Historical Society of Wisconsin*, compiled by Wissialm J. Schereck and Catherine Henke, December 1971. More than 1,500 entries. Available from Brown county Library, 515 Pine St., Green Bay WI 54301-5194.

WHERE TO GO

Barkhausen Sanctuary, 2024 Lakeview Drive, Suamico, WI 54173, managed by Brown County, is on the west shore of Green Bay between Peats Lake and Long Tail Point. It has ecological restoration and an information center.

Bay Beach Wildlife Sanctuary, Green Bay, is seven hundred acres located on the northeast side of the city of Green Bay. Phone (920) 391-3671. It has a waterfowl refuge, exhibit building, nature trails, hunting decoys, duck shack from the bay's west shore, and wooden duck skiffs. Deer and wild turkey roam free. Canada geese and mallard are common in large numbers during spring and fall. Black ducks and blue geese are often seen, also. It is the perfect environment for the budding naturalist.

Green Bay Shores State Wildlife Areas, managed by the Wisconsin Department of Natural Resources, include Long Tail Point, Peats Lake, Sensiba, Pensaukee, Oconto Marsh, and Peshtigo Harbor. Hunting is allowed in season. Contact the Department of Natural Resources, Green Bay [phone (920) 492-5800] for access information and names of guides.

Oshkosh Public Museum, 1331 Algoma Blvd., Oshkosh, WI 54901. Phone (920) 424-4730. Featuring exhibits on wetland restoration, the museum also has some area hunting decoys and displays that include renditions of duck hunting in the 1930s.

Thousand Islands Environmental Center, 1000 Beaulieu Court, Kaukauna, WI 54130. Phone (920) 766-4733. One of the most beautiful parts of the Fox River, the center has a waterfowl refuge, bald eagles, hiking trails, and a nature center on 325 acres. Lee W. Hammen is the naturalist.

Famous hunting areas in the southern Fox River region include Lake Butte des Mortes, Lake Poygan, Lake Winneconne, Rush Lake, Lake Puckaway, Lake Maria, and Buffalo Lake. Information about public access, hunting guides, and state wildlife areas is available through the Department of Natural Resources in Madison [phone (608) 266-2621 or (608) 266-8204].

ORGANIZATIONS

Ducks Unlimited, One Waterfowl Way, Memphis, TN 38120. Phone (901) 748-3825. Since 1937, this private nonprofit conservation organization has preserved more than 10 million acres of waterfowl habitat in North America.

Friends of the Fox, P.O. Box 741, Appleton, WI 54912-0741. This organization was founded in 1982 to preserve and develop the environmental and cultural assets of the Fox River system.

Green Bay Duck Hunters Association, P.O. Box 292, Suamico, WI 54173. Many of the region's most experienced hunters are members. New hunters are welcomed. Membership includes a newsletter about the Association's activities: building nesting structures, wetland restoration, decoy exhibits, and potluck suppers.

Wisconsin Waterfowl Association, P.O. Box 180496, Delafield, WI 53018. In addition to producing a member magazine, the Association is involved in wetland restoration projects, waterfowl conservation, and construction of nest structures for Canada geese, mallard, wood ducks, and other waterfowl.

SUPPLIERS

Parker, 2451 West Mason, P.O. Box 10886, Green Bay, WI 54307-0886. Founded in 1875 and still going strong is Parker, makers of paints for duck boats and decoys. The firm even furnishes illustrated instructions for painting canvasback, bluebill, geese, mallard, and other species.

The American Water Spaniel, the Wisconsin State Dog—retrieving ducks for Fox River hunters since the 1800s.

ILLUSTRATION CREDITS

Color photographs by Michael Brisson: pp. xv, xxi, 3, 4, 5, 8, 12, 15, 20, 22, 31, 33, 34 (left), 39, 40, 41, 44, 45, 46, 48, 50, 52 (upper and lower left), 55, 72, 73, 75.

Color photographs by Stephen Miller: pp. 28, 34 (right), 52 (upper right), 56.

Black-and-white photographs by Stephen Miller: pp. 10, 38, 78, 79, 80 (top), 81 through 93, 95 through 104, 105 (bottom), 106.

Color photographs by Philip Martin: pp. 27, 30.

Courtesy Jack and Carol Schmitz: color photographs (paintings by Milt Geyer) on pp. xii, 7, 9, 17, 19, 21; color photograph on p. xix; also historical black-and-white photos on pp. vii, viii, 23, 25, 52, (lower right), 80 (bottom).

Courtesy Earl Loyster: photos on pp. 58, 60, 61, 63, 66, 68.

Courtesy De Pere Historical Society: photo on p. 42.

Courtesy Area Research Center, University of Wisconsin-Green Bay: photo on p. xi

It ends like it began
rain over dry marsh
flight of birds

{ **Year** }

— *Stephen Miller*

Local Canada geese trade back and forth on the river throughout the year. Their numbers multiply during spring and fall, when tens of thousands more migrate through.

More Great Titles
from Trails Books

ACTIVITY GUIDES

Great Wisconsin Walks: 45 Strolls, Rambles, Hikes, and Treks, Wm. Chad McGrath

Great Minnesota Walks: 49 Strolls, Rambles, Hikes, and Treks, Wm. Chad McGrath

Acorn Guide to Northwest Wisconsin, Tim Bewer

Paddling Southern Wisconsin: 82 Great Trips by Canoe and Kayak, Mike Svob

Paddling Northern Wisconsin: 82 Great Trips by Canoe and Kayak, Mike Svob

Wisconsin Underground: A Guide to Caves, Mines, and Tunnels in and around the Badger State, Doris Green

Best Wisconsin Bike Trips, Phil Van Valkenberg

TRAVEL GUIDES

Historical Wisconsin Getaways: Touring the Badger State's Past, Sharyn Alden

The Great Wisconsin Touring Book: 30 Spectacular Auto Tours, Gary Knowles

Wisconsin Lighthouses: A Photographic and Historical Guide, Ken and Barb Wardius

Wisconsin Waterfalls, Patrick Lisi

Wisconsin Family Weekends: 20 Fun Trips for You and the Kids, Susan Lampert Smith

County Parks of Wisconsin, Revised Edition, Jeannette and Chet Bell

Up North Wisconsin: A Region for All Seasons, Sharyn Alden

The Spirit of Door County: A Photographic Essay, Darryl R. Beers

Great Wisconsin Taverns: 101 Distinctive Badger Bars, Dennis Boyer

Great Weekend Adventures, the Editors of Wisconsin Trails

The Wisconsin Traveler's Companion: A Guide to Country Sights, Jerry Apps and Julie Sutter-Blair

NATURE ESSAYS

Wild Wisconsin Notebook, James Buchholz

Trout Friends, Bill Stokes

Northern Passages: Reflections from Lake Superior Country, Michael Van Stappen

River Stories: Growing up on the Wisconsin, Delores Chamberlain

More Great Titles
from Trails Books
(continued)

HISTORICAL BOOKS

Prairie Whistles: Tales of Midwest Railroading,
Dennis Boyer

Barns of Wisconsin, Jerry Apps

Portrait of the Past: A Photographic Journey Through Wisconsin 1865-1920, Howard Mead, Jill Dean, and Susan Smith

Wisconsin: The Story of the Badger State,
Norman K. Risjord

GHOST STORIES

Haunted Wisconsin, Michael Norman and Beth Scott

W-Files: True Reports of Wisconsin's Unexplained Phenomena, Jay Rath

Northern Frights: A Supernatural Ecology of the Wisconsin Headwaters, Dennis Boyer

Giants in the Land: Folktales and Legends of Wisconsin, Dennis Boyer

For a free catalog, phone, write, or e-mail us.
Trails Books • P.O. Box 317, Black Earth, WI 53515
(800) 236-8088 • e-mail: info@wistrails.com
www.trailsbooks.com